My New School

Written by Kirsten Hall
Illustrated by Barry Gott

My First
READER

children's press®

A Division of Scholastic Inc.
New York Toronto London Auckland Sydney
Mexico City New Delhi Hong Kong
Danbury, Connecticut

Library of Congress Cataloging-in-Publication Data

Hall, Kirsten.
　My new school / written by Kirsten Hall ; illustrated by Barry Gott.
　　　p. cm. – (My first reader)
Summary: A young boy shows the reader, and someone hidden until the end, all around his school, pointing out the different rooms, demonstrating things he has learned to do, and sharing his favorite book.
　ISBN 0-516-24413-2 (lib. bdg.)　　0-516-25505-3 (pbk.)
　[1. Schools–Fiction. 2. Brothers–Fiction. 3. Stories in rhyme.] I. Gott, Barry, ill. II. Title. III. Series.
　PZ8.3.H146Myc 2004
　[E]–dc22

　　　　　　　　　　　　2003014070

Published in 2004 by Children's Press, an imprint of Scholastic Library Publishing.
Published simultaneously in Canada.
Printed in the United States of America.

CHILDREN'S PRESS and associated logos are trademarks and or
registered trademarks of Scholastic Library Publishing. SCHOLASTIC and
associated logos are trademarks and or registered trademarks of Scholastic Inc.

1 2 3 4 5 6 7 8 9 10 R 13 12 11 10 09 08 07 06 05 04

Note to Parents and Teachers

Once a reader can recognize and identify the 33 words used to tell this story, he or she will be able to successfully read the entire book. These 33 words are repeated throughout the story, so that young readers will be able to recognize the words easily and understand their meaning.

The 33 words used in this book are:

again	I	play	turn
art	is	read	where
better	learn	room	will
can	let's	school	write
count	letters	soon	you
day	much	ten	your
draw	my	the	
every	new	this	
get	now	to	

This is my new school.

This is where I play.

This is the art room.

I draw every day!

This is where I count.

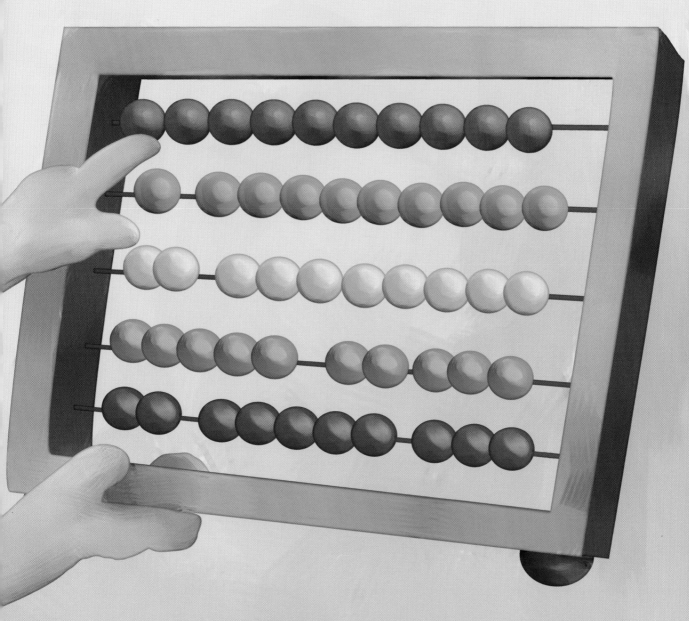

I can count to ten.

This is where I read.

Let's read this again!

This is where I write.

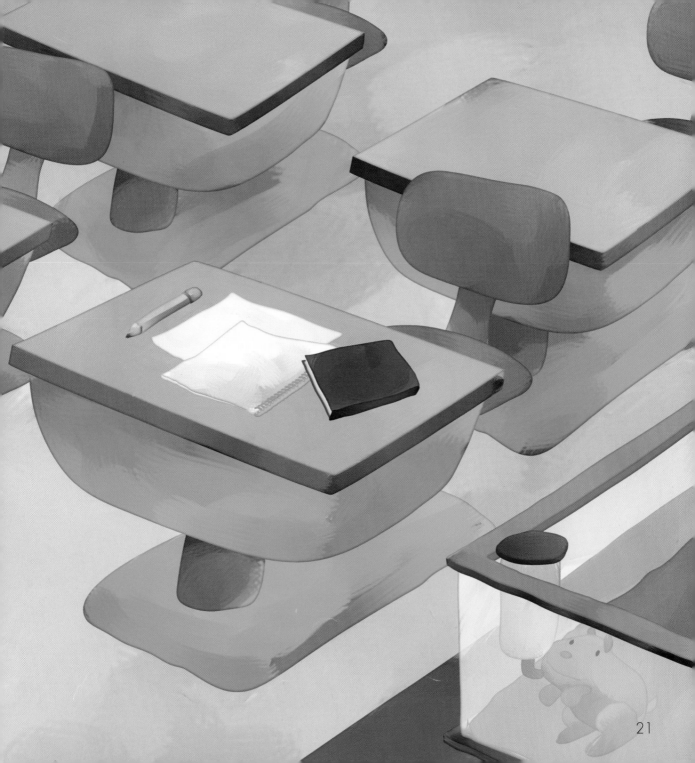

ABCDEFGH
IJKLMNOP
QRSTUVW
XYZ

I can write my letters.

cat sat
mat rat
bat bat

I write every day.

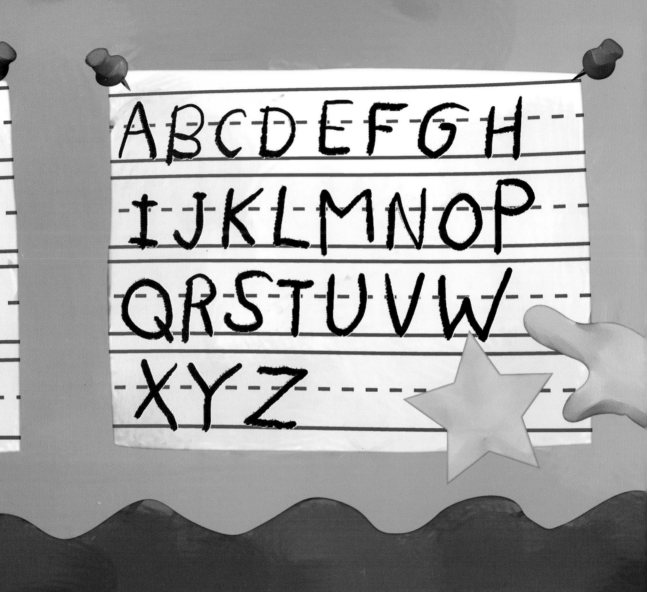

Now I write much better!

This is where I learn.

Soon you will get your turn.

ABOUT THE AUTHOR

Kirsten Hall has lived most of her life in New York City. While she was still in high school, she published her first book for children, *Bunny, Bunny*. Since then, she has written and published more than sixty children's books. Hall hopes that by reading this book, new students everywhere will feel less nervous about starting school. A former early education teacher, Hall currently works as a children's book editor.

ABOUT THE ILLUSTRATOR

Barry Gott used to work in a big office writing and drawing hundreds of greeting cards. These days he works from his home, illustrating children's books. He doesn't miss driving on the freeway every morning, but he does miss the french fry vending machine. Gott lives in South Euclid, Ohio.